VAN HALEN

II

AUTHENTIC GUITAR TAB EDITION

Alfred Publishing Co., Inc.
16320 Roscoe Blvd., Suite 100
P.O. Box 10003
Van Nuys, CA 91410-0003
alfred.com

Copyright © MMVII by Alfred Publishing Co., Inc.
All rights reserved. Printed in USA.

ISBN-10: 0-7390-4999-2
ISBN-13: 978-0-7390-4999-0

VAN HALEN
II

ALBUM NOTES

Release Date: May 23, 1979
Top Chart Position: No. 6 (over 5 million copies sold to date)
Standout Tracks: "Dance the Night Away" and "Beautiful Girls"
Significance: Expanded Van Halen's audience with the commercial success of the singles "Dance the Night Away" and "Beautiful Girls."

VAN HALEN II

FOREWORD

Van Halen II is a continuation of the cocky, strutting style of rock established on the band's debut album. The pyrotechnical electric guitar display of "Eruption" has been replaced by the acoustic virtuoso showcase of "Spanish Fly." The role of a heavier remake of a '60s hit filled by "You Really Got Me" on the debut is assumed by the plodding cover of "You're No Good" on *Van Halen II*. Eddie Van Halen's now famous "brown sound" is combined with his effortless fretboard facility to impressive effect on the heavy riffs in "Somebody Get Me a Doctor" and "D.O.A." and the boogie shuffle of "Bottoms Up!" On a lighter side, the tapped harmonics on the introduction of "Women in Love…" produces a lovely hammered dulcimer effect. The band revealed a pop side of their sound with the thick vocal harmonies and melodic hooks in the catchy original anthems "Beautiful Girls" and "Dance the Night Away," both becoming Top 10 hits.

VAN HALEN II

CONTENTS

YOU'RE NO GOOD	5
DANCE THE NIGHT AWAY	11
SOMEBODY GET ME A DOCTOR	20
BOTTOMS UP!	25
OUTTA LOVE AGAIN	33
LIGHT UP THE SKY	38
SPANISH FLY	47
D.O.A.	50
WOMEN IN LOVE...	58
BEAUTIFUL GIRLS	64

YOU'RE NO GOOD

Words and Music by
CLINT BALLARD, JR.

N.C.
Chorus
E5
*8va
real - ly are. You're no good!
ah.)
(No good, no good. Ba - by, you're no good.
8va
Full
loco
sl.
P.M.
*8va applies to lead vocal only (throughout).
Ooh, yeah.
No good, no good, no good.
Oh
semi-harm.
1/2
1/4
P
no!
Ba - by, you're no good.)
1½
trem. bar
2nd Verse
N.C.
I broke her heart, sim - ple and true. Broke her heart for

Pre-chorus
F5
G
Csus2
some - one like you.
If you're com - in' back, don't come run - ning to me.
(Oh, oh, oh.
let ring
sl.
P
Asus2
Dsus2
E5
N.C.
8va
I wan - na love you, may - be set you free.
Ah, ah, ah.)
Oh no!
(You're no good,
P.M.
mp
f
Full
Chorus
loco
no good, no good. Ba - by, you're no good.
Woh.
Oh no!
You're no good, no good, no good.
Oh good.
T
*Vib. w/L.H.

no!
Ba - by, you're no good.)
Ha!
loco
trem. bar
P.M.
A.H.
Guitar solo
N.C.
reverse rake
vib. w/bar
*Glide up and down D stg. w/side of right hand (lightly touching it) while hammering on and pulling off with left hand, sounding random harmonics and muted notes.
vib. w/L.H.
*Bend at 8th fret w/L.H.
*Bend at 7th fret w/L.H.
*Bend at 7th fret w/L.H.
grad. bend
*Bend at 8th fret w/L.H.

*Bend at 7th fret w/L.H. Hold bend w/tapping finger and quickly move L.H. to 10th fret for pull-off.

(Spoken:) Used to be I couldn't sleep at night, baby.

Now, you go on and do what you want to.

Ow!

Oh no! Oh
(No good, no good, no good.

8va
no!
Ba - by, you're no good.)
Ow!
Oh no!
Full
sl.
loco
P.M.
A5
G
C5
w/Fill 1
Ah.
Gtr. II
1½
trem. bar
rit.
Gtr. I
H P
Fill 1
Gtr. III

DANCE THE NIGHT AWAY

Words and Music by
EDWARD VAN HALEN, ALEX VAN HALEN,
MICHAEL ANTHONY and DAVID LEE ROTH

Tune down 1/2 step:
⑥ = Eb ③ = Gb
⑤ = Ab ② = Bb
④ = Db ① = Eb

E B A E Esus4 E A B
cross the room. Yes, it's love in the third de - gree.
P.M. P.M. P.M. sl.
Pre-chorus
B5 C♯5 B C♯5 B5
Ooh. Won't ya turn your head my way?
(Ooh, ba - by, ba - by.)
P.M. P.M. sl.
C♯5 B
Ooh Ah, come on!
(Ooh, ba - by, ba - by.)
P P.M.
C♯m B Bsus4 B Bsus4
Take a chance. You're old e - nough to dance
P.M. P.M.

Chorus
E
Esus4
E B A E Esus4
(Dance the night a - way.
the night a - way.
Riff A
(Gtr. II)
8va
loco
sl.
clean tone w/flanger
*Tapped harmonics. Fret note normally and tap directly on fret indicated in parentheses, using R.H. index finger.
Gtr. I
P.M.
E A B E Esus4 E B A E
Ooh, oh.
Come on, g - girl, dance the night a - way.
Ah, dance the night a - way.)
*Sound open stg. by tapping ⑥ at top of fretboard.
P.M.----

2nd Verse
Esus4
E A B E
Esus4
A live wire.
Bare -
(end Riff A)
8va
loco
8va
T
sl.
(Gtr. II out)
P.M.
E B A E
Esus4
E A B E
ly a be - gin - ner, but just watch that la - dy go.
She's on
Esus4
E B A E
Esus4
E A B N.C.
fire 'cause danc - in' gets her high - er than, uh, an - y - thing else she knows.

Pre-chorus
B5 C♯5 B C♯5 B5
Ooh.___ Won't ya___ turn your head my___ way?___
(Ooh, ba - by, ba - by.)
P.M.
sl.
pick slide
H
C♯5 B
Ooh.___ Well, don't
(Ooh, ba - by, ba - by.)
P
C♯m B Bsus4 B Bsus4
skip ro - mance,___ 'cause you're old e - nough to dance___
Chorus
w/Riff A
E Esus4 E B A E Esus4
the night___ a - way.___
(Dance___ the night___ a - way.___
P.M.
sl.

16

*Tapped harmonics, as before. For 'A' and 'B' chords, angle R.H. index finger to correspond to L.H. chord shape.

*Tap ⑥ at 16th fret, sounding both the harmonic

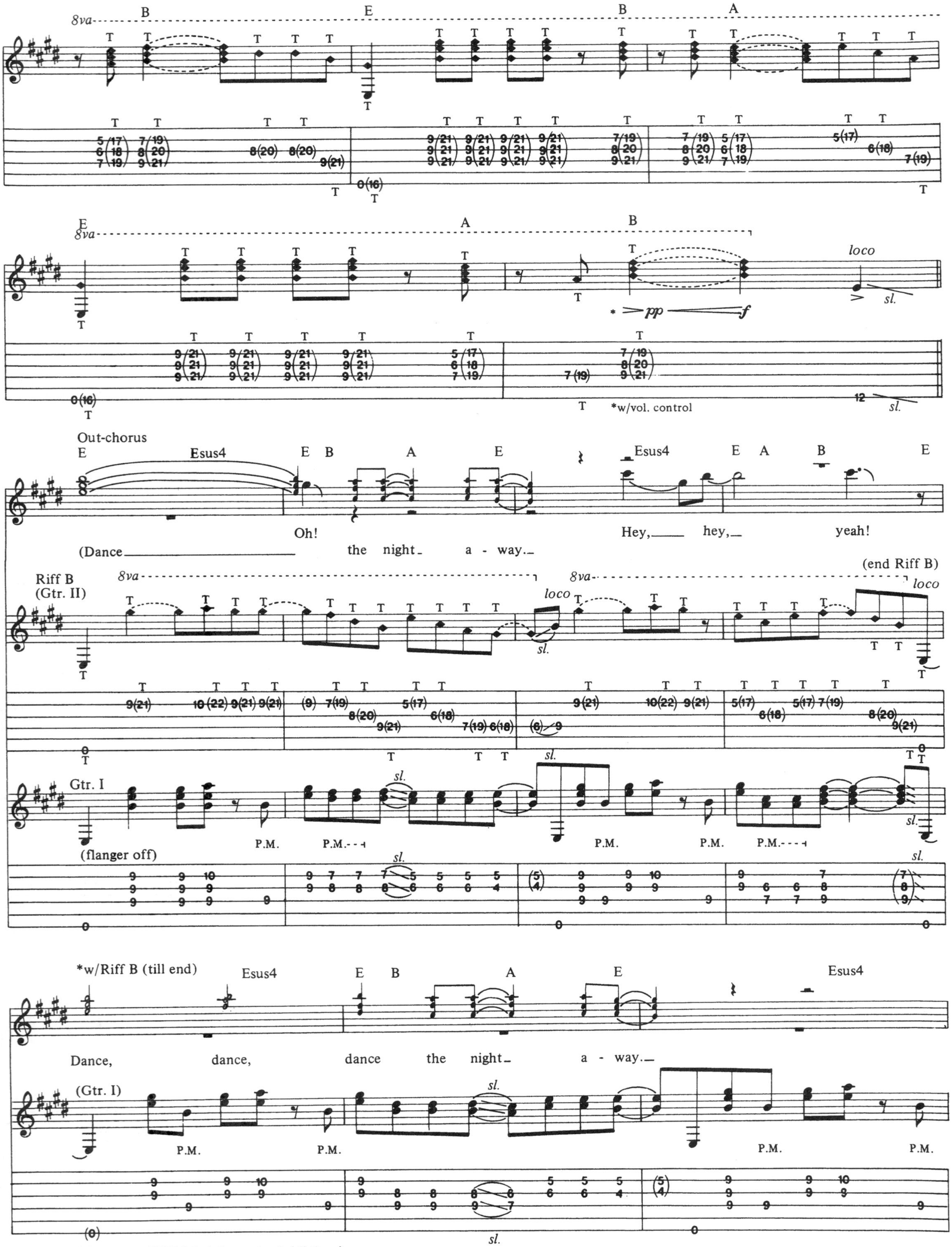

*First note of Riff B is tied, not struck (all times).

E A B E Esus4 E B A E
Ah, come on, ba - by.
Dance the night a - way.
P.M.
sl.
P.M.
Esus4 E A B E Esus4 E B A E
Hey, hey, yeah!
Dance, dance, dance the night a - way.
P.M.
sl.
P.M.
Begin fade
Esus4 E A B E Esus4 E B A E
Ah, come on, ba - by, ba - by, yeah.
Dance the night a - way.
Ooh,
P.M. P.M. P.M.
sl.
P.M.
Fade out
Esus4 E A B E Esus4 E B A E
ooh, yeah.
Dance, dance dance the night a - way.)
Ah,
P.M.
sl.
P.M.

SOMEBODY GET ME A DOCTOR

Words and Music by
EDWARD VAN HALEN, ALEX VAN HALEN,
MICHAEL ANTHONY and DAVID LEE ROTH

Tune down ½ step:
⑥ = E♭ ③ = G♭
⑤ = A♭ ② = B♭
④ = D♭ ① = E♭

1st Verse
E F E F
call me a doc - tor. Feel - in' no pain. O - ver - load - ed, down the
Harm. P.M. Harm.
pick. sl. H sl.
Chorus
w/Riff A (2 times)
N.C.(A5) Dsus4 D N.C.(A5) Dsus4 D
drain. Some - bod - y get me a doc - tor. You bet - ter
2nd Verse
E F E F
call up the am - bu - lance. I'm deep in shock. O - ver load - ed, ba - by. I can hard - ly
Harm. P.M. Harm.
pick. sl. H sl.
Chorus
w/Riff A (3 times)
N.C.(A5) Dsus4 D N.C.(A5)
walk. Some - bod - y get me a doc - tor. Oo!
Dsus4 D N.C.(A5) Dsus4 D
Some - bod - y get me a doc - tor. Yeah!
3rd Verse
E F F♯
I'm feel - in' o - ver - fine, and I'm speed - in'
P.M.

G
N.C.(A5)
down _ that _ line. _
(Whispered:) Ah. _
* off f
*Fade in w/volume control.
Whoo! Whoo! _
off f
semi. harm. trem. bar
Guitar solo
N.C.(B5)
trem. bar
*Push stg. into pickup pole piece.

(G5)
Full
(F5)
1/2
sl.
P
(G5)
(B♭5)
(C5)
(D5)
(E5)
Harm.
(8va)
P.M.
non-harm.
(B♭5)
(C5)
(D5)
Free time
E5
rit.
trem. bar w/applause & cheers
Fdbk.
(8va)
slack
trem. bar
Fdbk. pitch: G
Tempo I
w/Riff A (3 times)
N.C.(A5)
Dsus4 D
N.C.(A5)
Dsus4 D
N.C.(A5)
Dsus4 D
Oo!
w/Indian war whoops.
N.C.
rake
*Glide up and down 6th stg. w/side of right hand (lightly touching it) while hammering on and pulling off with left hand, sounding random muted notes and harmonics.
**R.H. slide
*Pull off from 4th fret (held from previous bar).
w/Riff A (2 times)
N.C.(A5)
Dsus4 D
N.C.(A5)
Dsus4 D
Ow!
Ooh.
Ya bet - ter

4th Verse
E
F
E5
E
call up the doc - tor,
feel - in' high!
I'm o - ver - load - ed, ba - by.
P.M.
P.M.
P.M.
F
Chorus
w/Riff A (3½ times)
N.C.(A5)
Dsus4 D
N.C.(A5)
I say,
bye bye,
(Some-bod - y get me a doc - tor.
Oh,
pick slides
Dsus4 D
N.C.(A5)
Dsus4 D
N.C.(A5)
8va
yeah.
Ooh,
ooh.
Ah,
Some-bod - y get me a doc - tor.
Some-bod - y get me a doc - tor.)
Free time
8va
Dsus4
D
8va
loco
N.C. (A5)
yeah!
Oo!
Some bod - y give me a shot!
Fdbk.
sl.
rit.
Fdbk.
sl.
Fdbk. pitches: A
A

BOTTOMS UP!

Words and Music by
EDWARD VAN HALEN, ALEX VAN HALEN,
MICHAEL ANTHONY and DAVID LEE ROTH

© 1979 VAN HALEN MUSIC and DIAMOND DAVE MUSIC
This Arrangement © 1992 VAN HALEN MUSIC and DIAMOND DAVE MUSIC
All Rights for VAN HALEN MUSIC Administered by WB MUSIC CORP.
All Rights Reserved

1st, 2nd Verses
w/Rhy. Fig. 1
A5
C5
A5
sit - ting here — 'bout half the night, — uh. Uh, ma - ma, fill my cup —
2. See additional lyrics
D5
A5
C5
— up. Said I came here — to waste — some time. —
A5
N.C.(D5)
(C♯5)
(C5)
Pre-chorus
Gtr. I
B5 A5 B5 A5 B5 A5 B5 C5
I think I'm — gon - na jump - up. — I'm sing - in', I'm danc - in'
(cont. in slashes)
P
A5 B5 A5 B5 A5 B5 C5
sl.
D5 E5 D5 E5 D5 E5 G5
3
3
most ev - er - y night. — And I want to do — that with you, babe.
To Coda
E5 D5 E5 D5 E5
⑥12fr.
E
Chorus
w/Rhy. Fig. 1 (1st 5 bars only)
A5
Let's do this bot - tle right! —
(Oh, —
C5
A5
D5
A5
Oh, oh, — ba - by! — Oh! — Bot - toms up! —
ba - by!) —
(cont. in notation)
G5 G♯5 A5 N.C.
D.S. al Coda
Ow! - Harm. Whoo!
sl.
3
Harm.
Coda
⑥12fr.
E
sl.
bot - tle right! —

Guitar solo
F#5
Gtr. II
w/flanger
1/2
P
Full
N.C.
sl.
H P
Gtr. I
F#5
H P sl. H H P H H P H
B5
1/4
A.H.
(15ma)
Full 1/2
A.H. pitch: D#
N.C.
*straight 8ths
N.C.(A5)
(Gtr. II out)
Fdbk.
(8va)
dim.
*Band continues triplet feel.
Fdbk. pitch: F#

Interlude
N.C.
Uh, ha, ha, ha, ha, ha, ha, ha! Whoo! Ah. Uh, alright!
Gtr. I
mp
w/fingers
Ow! Edward, sing a little bit, yeah!
Rhy. Fig. 2
(end Rhy. Fig. 2)
w/Rhy. Fig. 2 (3½ times)
Come-um - um - um - um - um, ba - by, bot - toms up.
Come-um - um - um - um - um, ba - by,
bot - toms up.
Come-um - um - um - um - um, ba - by,
whoo, bot - toms up. Bum, bum, bah. Let'scome-um - um - um - um - um, ba - by,

29

A5
Harm.
Gtr. II (8va)
C5
(w/flanger)
trem. bar
semi-harm.
Gtr. I
sl.
let ring
H
P
D5
P.M.
rake
Rhy. Fig. 2
w/Rhy. Fig. 2 (1½ times)
8va
*Push stg. into pickup polepiece.
(end Rhy. Fig. 2)

8va - - - loco
C5
A5
D5
grad. bend
*Straight 8ths.
A5
C5
N.C.
trem. pick
(Gtr. I)
A5
C5
A5
(Gtr. II out)
trem. bar (slow dive)
pick slide
pick scrape
pick scrape
*Don't pick.

Additional Lyrics

2. Pretty maids all in a row. Go on, set 'em up, up.
   Uh, come - um - um - um - um - um, ba - by, bottoms up! *(To Pre-chorus)*

OUTTA LOVE AGAIN

Words and Music by
EDWARD VAN HALEN, ALEX VAN HALEN,
MICHAEL ANTHONY and DAVID LEE ROTH

Wow! Deal - in' with your troub - les drove me a -
semi - harm.
H
sl.
way, yeah, yeah.
Yeah!
D5 E5
Oh well, uh,
(end Rhy. Fig. 1)
Chorus
B5 C5 C♯5
C5 C♯5 D5
C♯5 D5 D♯5
say - in' that you're leav - in'. I don't wan - na hear that talk. Stare at dis - be - lief in me when
Rhy. Fig. 2
D5 D♯5 E5 B♭5 A5
E5 B♭5 A5
E5
I just up and walk out - ta love.
(Out - ta love.) a -
P
H

Bb5 A5
E5
Bb5 A5
gain.
(Out - ta love.)
Ah, ow!
P H
E5
Bb5 A5
E5
Once a - gain.
(Whispered:) Ah.
(end Rhy. Fig. 2)
pick sl.
H P H
Interlude
N.C.(E5)
A.H.
(15ma)
(8va)
semi-harm.
P.M.
A.H. pitch: E
C♯
B
A
E
G
Ooh,
1/2
3/4

2nd Verse
w/Rhy. Fig. 1
N.C.(E5)
love me now, love me now, treat me like a fool! Did you?
Did you? I mean you're do - in' all you can to make me sad and blue, yeah, yeah.
Chorus
w/Rhy. Fig. 2
D5 E5 B5 C5 C♯5
Did you? Uh! Oh well, oh, say - in' you are leav - in'. I don't
C5 C♯5 D5 C♯5 D5 D♯5 D5 D♯5 E5 B♭5 A5
wan - na hear that talk. Stare at dis - be - lief in me when I just up and walk
E5 B♭5 A5 E5
out - ta love, (Out - ta love.) a -
B♭5 A5 E5 B♭5 A5
gain. (Out - ta love.) Wah.
E5 B♭5 A5 E5
Wow! Once a - gain.
Guitar solo
N.C.(E5)
8va
loco
sl.
P
H
Full
P.M.
1/2
1½

3rd Verse
w/Rhy. Fig. 1
N.C.(E5)

Love me now, love me now, you treat me like a fool. Woh! Tell you. Ooh. Tell you. Yeah. Doin' all you can to make me sad and blue, ow!

Chorus
w/Rhy. Fig. 2

Did you? Yeah. Oh, you're talkin' 'bout your leavin'. I don't wanna hear that talk. Stare at disbelief in me when I just up and walk out of love a-(Outta love.) gain, a-(Outta love.) g- g- g- g- gain, ow!

Outta Love Again - 5 - 5

LIGHT UP THE SKY

Words and Music by
EDWARD VAN HALEN, ALEX VAN HALEN,
MICHAEL ANTHONY and DAVID LEE ROTH

Light Up the Sky - 9 - 2

Pre - chorus
2nd time substitute Rhy. Fill 2
Em
I watch my tel - e - vi - sion, al - most lost my
P.M.
Csus2
2nd time substitute Rhy. Fill 3
mind. It said, "O - pen your eyes.
P
let ring
H H
F5
N.C.
F5 D5 F5 D5
Leave it all be - hind."
H P
pick slide
P.M.
P.M.

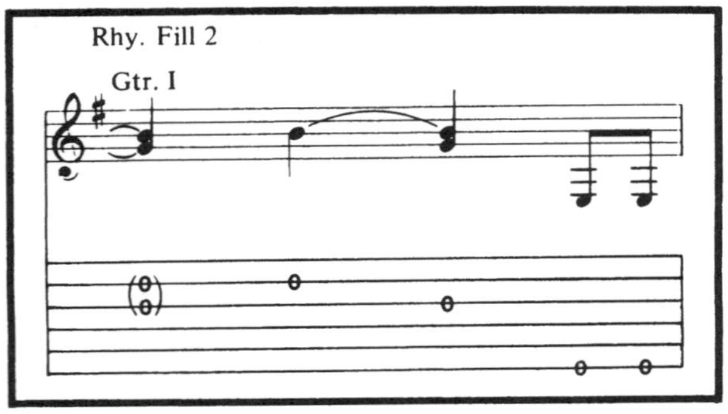
Rhy. Fill 2
Gtr. I

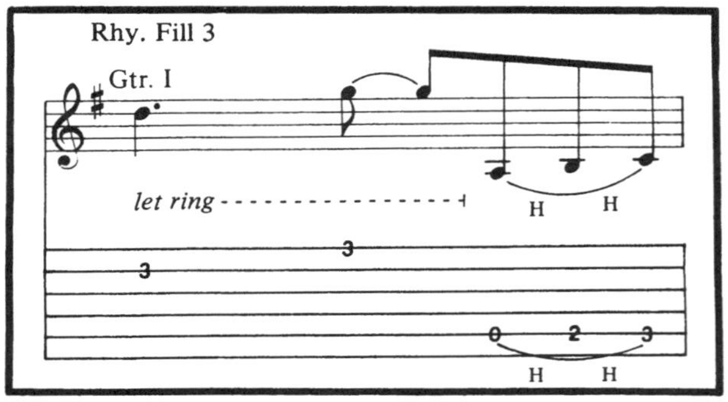
Rhy. Fill 3
Gtr. I
let ring
H H

Light Up the Sky - 9 - 4

2.
Dsus4 D
C5
F5
Esus4
skies. You won't rec - og - nize them an - y -
H
let ring
E
Bridge
*N.C.(A)
more.
Ooh,
mp
P.M.
*Chords implied by bass gtr. (next 15 bars).
(D)
(E)
ma - ma, see the fire - light.
P
sl.
(A)
(D)
(E)
Ooh, we're com - in' out to - night.
*P
*Pull off from G♯(② 9 fr.).

Light Up the Sky - 9 - 6

D♯5 D5 C5
D5 D♯5 E5
P.M.
Full
P H
1½
1
sl.
P
1/2
A.H.
(15ma)
trem. bar
grad. release
A.H. pitch: E
semi-harm.
Full
G5
E5(type 2)
rake
Drum solo
(Tacet)
12
N.C.
Gtr. I
mp
w/flanger
1.- 4.
5.
E5 D♯5 D5 C5
(cont. in slashes)
f
(flanger off)

45

Additional Lyrics

2. Wolves at my door, I wised up quick.
Turned here and gone from on the go.
Seemed the old folks who come up short
Were the pretty little kids who didn't wanna know.

2nd Pre-chorus: I had some crazy vision, one I can't deny.
And it said, "Open my eyes. Leave it all behind." *(To Chorus)*

SPANISH FLY

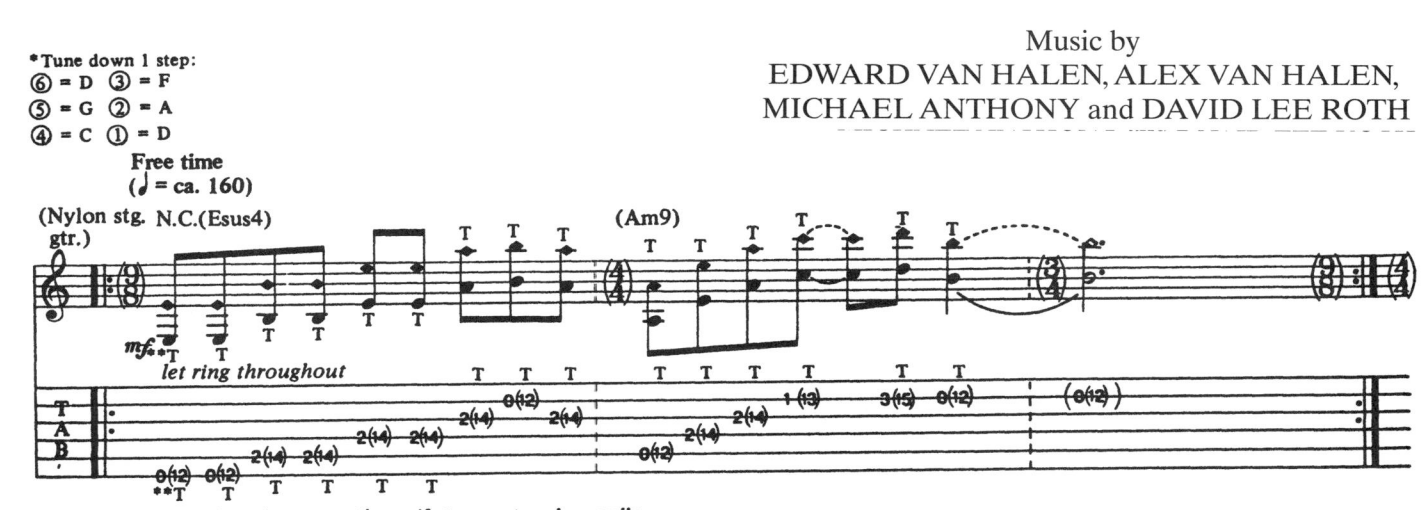

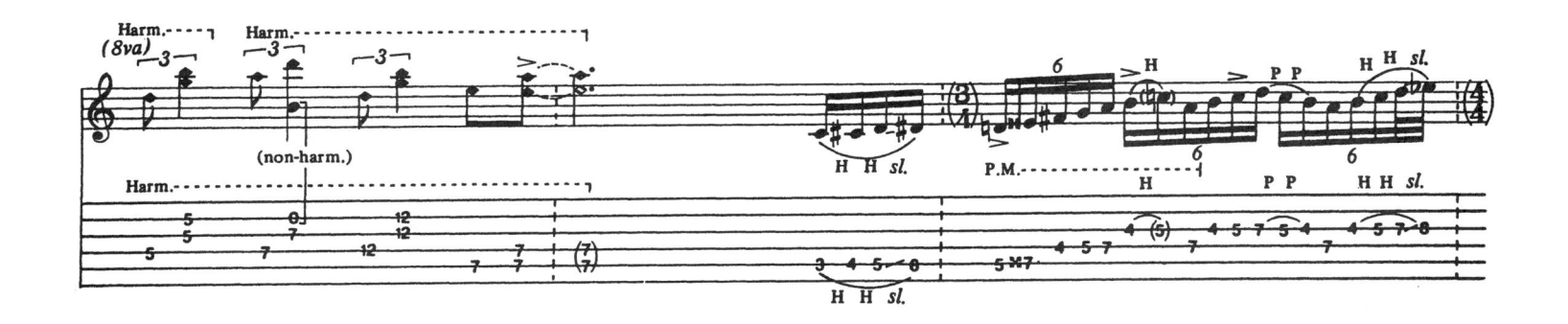

Music by
EDWARD VAN HALEN, ALEX VAN HALEN,
MICHAEL ANTHONY and DAVID LEE ROTH

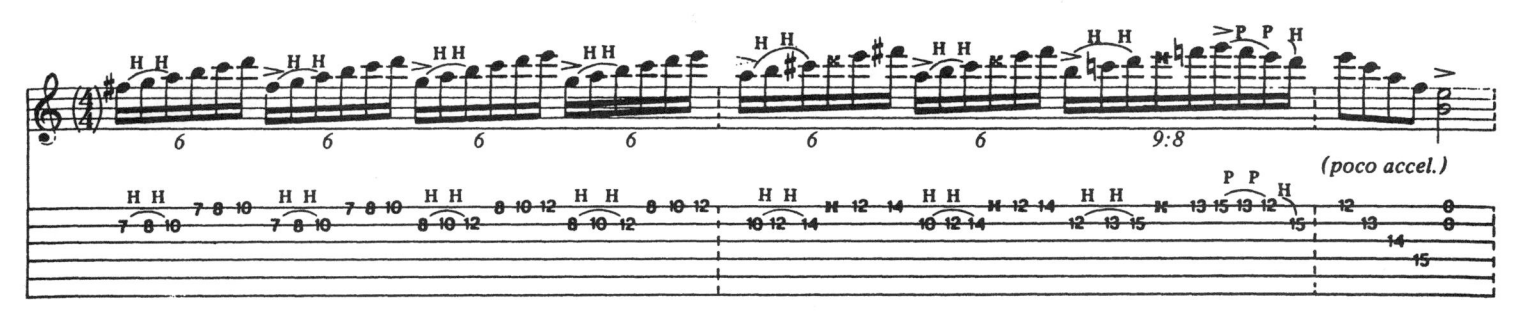

48

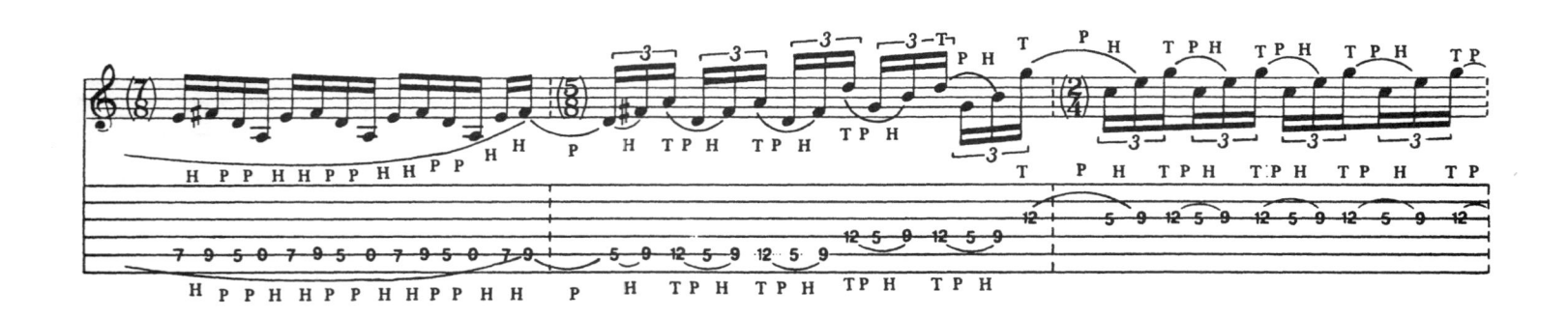

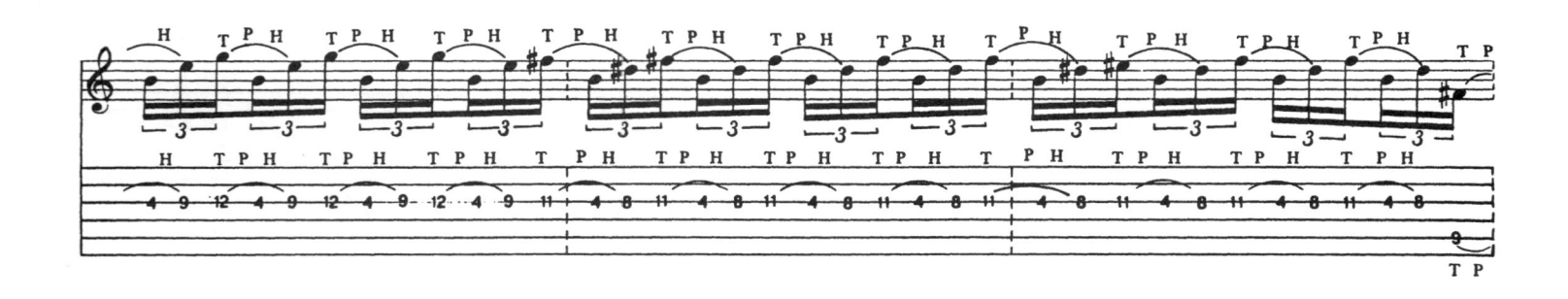

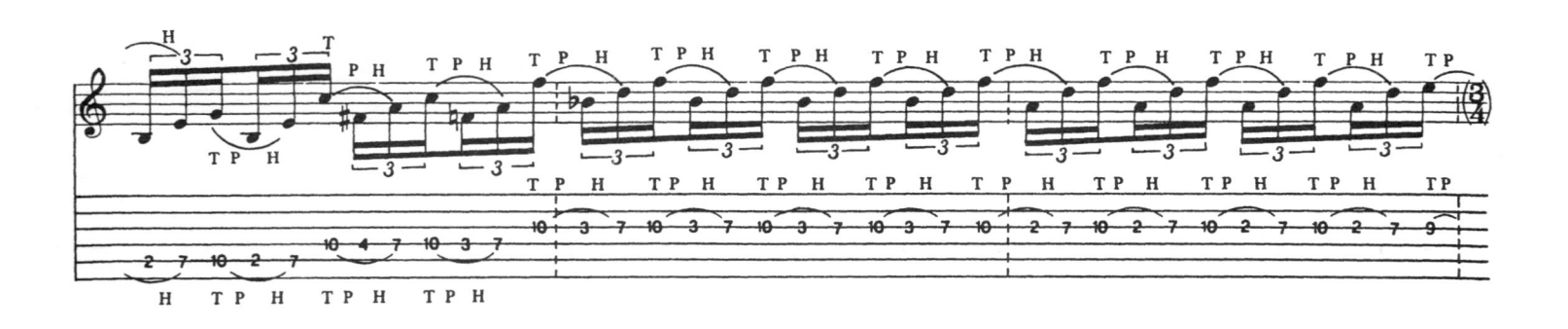

Spanish Fly - 3 - 3

D.O.A.

Words and Music by
EDWARD VAN HALEN, ALEX VAN HALEN,
MICHAEL ANTHONY and DAVID LEE ROTH

© 1979 VAN HALEN MUSIC and DIAMOND DAVE MUSIC
This Arrangement © 1992 VAN HALEN MUSIC and DIAMOND DAVE MUSIC
All Rights for VAN HALEN MUSIC Administered by WB MUSIC CORP.
All Rights Reserved

2nd time substitute Fill 1
3rd time substitute Fill 2
A5 N.C.
sher - iff down to try and drive us a - way.
We was
trem. pick
sl.
w/Rhy. Fig. 1
sit - tin' ducks for the po - lice - man.
They found a
2nd time to Coda I
3rd time to Coda II
dirt - y - faced kid in a gar - bage can, ha! Ooh.
T P H
(A5) (B5)
Pre-chorus
C#5
D5
And I'm a - lone, I'm on the high - way,
trem. bar
Fill 1
Full
P
T
grad. release
vib. w/ L.H.
*Release to 1/2.
Fill 2
1/2
A.H. (15ma)
Full 1/2
H
1½
sl. P
trem. bar

C♯5
D5
E5
Chorus
A5
N.C.
want - ed
dead or a - live,
(Dead or a - live.)
sl.
A5 N.C.
A5 N.C.
A5 N.C.
D.S. al Coda I
dead or a - live.
1/2
A.H.
(15ma)
semi - harm.
trem. bar
1½
P
A.H. pitches: D♯ D
Coda I
A5 N.C.
A5 N.C.
(A5) (B5)
"Out - ta luck."
Ooh yeah.
T P H
T
Pre-chorus
C♯5
D5
N.C.
C♯5
D5
E5
And I'm a - lone,
I'm on the high - way,
want - ed
dead or a - live,
(Dead or a - live.)

Chorus
A5 N.C.
dead or a - live.
Ow!
trem. bar
Guitar solo I
*E5
A5 F♯5
semi - harm.
*Chords implied by bass gtr. (next 13 bars).
grad. bend
reverse rake
E5
Full
sl.
A5 F♯5 A5 B5 C♯5
D5

C♯5
N.C.
A5
Full
trem. bar
sl. sl.
P
A5 N.C.
D.S. al Coda II
Al - right!
Unh!
3. Now, I'm
steady gliss.
Coda II
(A5) (B5)
gar - bage can.
Ba - by, yeah, yeah.
grad. bend
Pre-chorus
C♯5
D5
Babe, I'm a - lone and I'm on the high - way,
want - ed

D5 E5
Chorus
A5 N.C.
A5 N.C.
A5 N.C.
dead or a - live,
(Dead or a - live.)
dead or a - live.
sl.
A5 N.C. (A5) (B5)
Ow, ow!
Guitar solo II
*C♯5
D5
Wow!
Full
slack
trem. bar
C♯5
*Chords implied by bass gtr. (next 12 bars).
N.C.
A5 F♯5
I'm gone!
1/2
P
trem. pick
A5 F♯5
A5 F♯5
N.C.
Ooh yeah.
Ooh!
A.H.
(15ma)
1½
rake
vib. w/bar
H P
P H
A.H. pitch: G♯

A5 F#5 A5 F#5
trem. bar
rake
A5 F#5 N.C.
Al - right!
sl.
semi - harm.
vib. w/bar
trem. bar
Outro
w/Rhy. Fig. 1 (2 times)
A5 N.C.
grad. accel.
Leav - in' down the road.
Yeah, yeah.
I'm a spark on the ho - ri - zon.
Ow!
Rhy. Fig. 2
(end Rhy. Fig. 2)

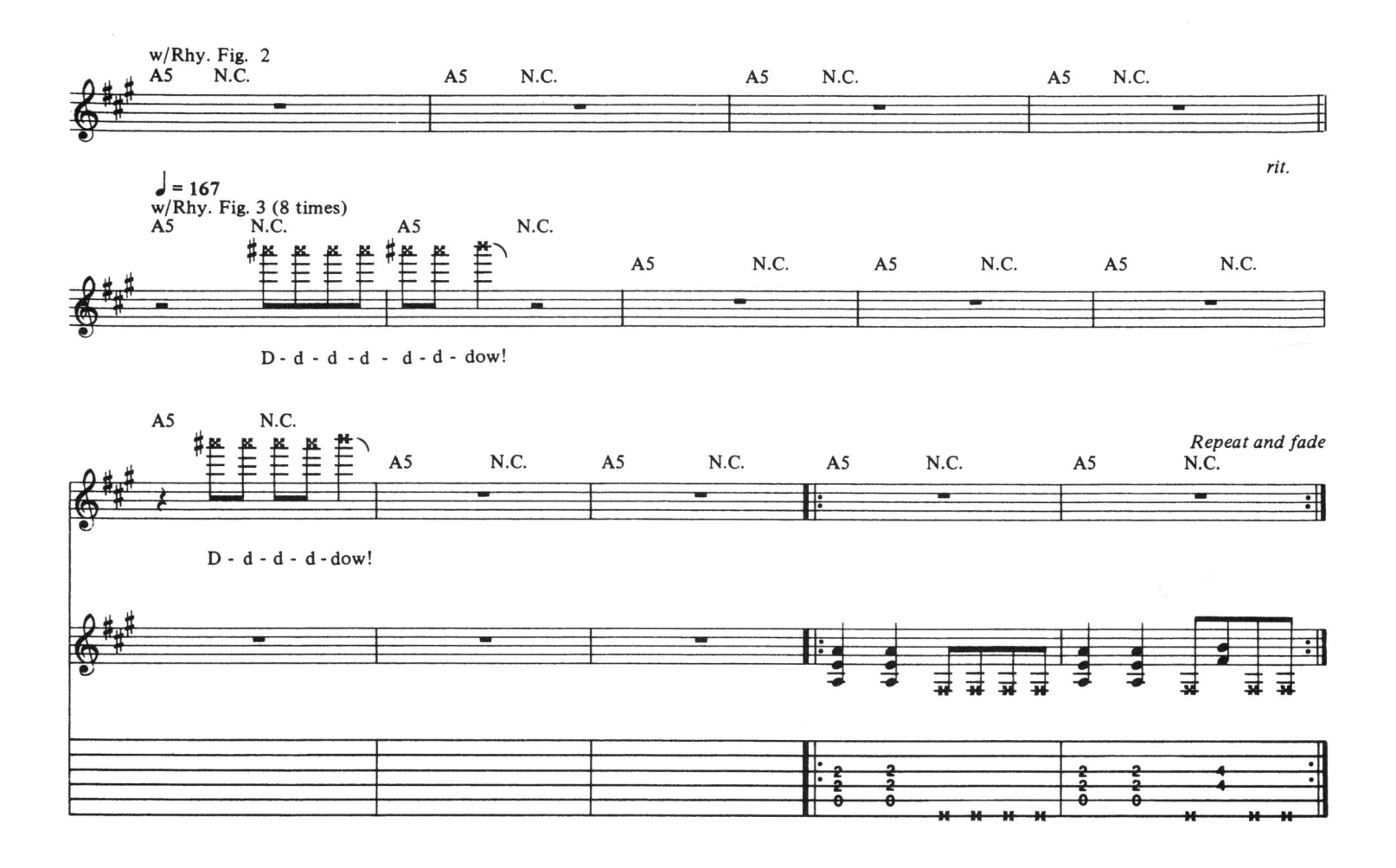

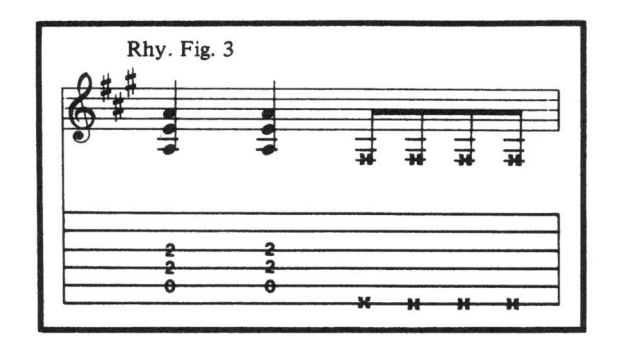

Additional Lyrics

2. Broken down and dirty, dressed in rags
   A-from the day my mama told me, "Boy, you pack your bags."
   I'll send the mayor down in his pickup truck.
   The jury look at me, say, "Outta luck." *(To Pre-chorus)*

3. Now, I'm broken down and dirty, dressed in rags
   A-from the day my mama told me, "Boy, you pack your bags."
   And we was sittin' ducks for the policeman.
   They found a dirty-faced kid in a garbage can.
   Baby, yeah, yeah! *(To Pre-chorus)*

WOMEN IN LOVE...

Words and Music by
EDWARD VAN HALEN, ALEX VAN HALEN,
MICHAEL ANTHONY and DAVID LEE ROTH

Tune down 1/2 step:
- ⑥ = Eb   ③ = Gb
- ⑤ = Ab   ② = Bb
- ④ = Db   ① = Eb

Moderate Rock ♩ = 104

*Gtr. II doubles Gtr. I, starting an eighth note later, creating an echo effect (next 4 bars).
**Tapped harmonics. Hold chord forms and tap stgs. at frets indicated in parentheses.
***Slide L.H. only.

Women in Love... - 6 - 1

© 1979 VAN HALEN MUSIC and DIAMOND DAVE MUSIC
This Arrangement © 1992 VAN HALEN MUSIC and DIAMOND DAVE MUSIC
All Rights for VAN HALEN MUSIC Administered by WB MUSIC CORP.
All Rights Reserved

Am/E
E5
N.C.
E7(no 3rd)
A/E
Am/E
E5
N.C.
(end Rhy. Fig. 1)
1st Verse
Am7(no 3rd)
Dadd4/A
Dmadd4/A
My heart, you're break - in' my heart. Girl, you bet - ter start think - in' some - thin' real.
Rhy. Fig. 2
let ring
A5
Am7(no 3rd)
Dadd4/A
Seems like lov - in' you is just a cra - zy dream,
let ring

Dmadd4/A
A5
N.C.
but do as you feel.
(end Rhy. Fig. 2)
sl.
let ring
let ring
sl.
Pre-chorus
Dadd2
E5
N.C.
C
D
N.C.
All these cra - zy wom - en,
one more cra - zy night.
But
Rhy. Fig. 3
*Harm.
*Harm.
sl.
let ring
*Lift pinky off 4th stg. to play harm. Let rest of chord ring.
Dadd2
E5
N.C.
C
D
N.C.
one night's all we're giv - en,
so ba - by,
leave me a - lone
or, la - dy,
stay the night.
(Ah,
ah.)
*Harm.
*T
T
sl.
P.M.
*Tapped harmonics

Chorus
w/Rhy. Fig. 1
E7(no 3rd)
A/E
Am/E
E5
Oh ba - by, make up your mind, uh.
(Oh, wom - en in love. Make up your mind.
N.C.
E7(no 3rd)
To Coda
A/E
Am/E
I know you're in love.
Oh, wom - en in love.
So ba - by, make up your mind.
E5
N.C.
2nd Verse
w/Rhy. Fig. 2
Am7(no 3rd)
Wom - en in love.)
Scream, ah! Go on and scream
Dadd4/A
Dmadd4/A
Substitute Rhy. Fill 1
A5
N.C.
that your love is all you're know - in'. But
Resume Rhy. Fig. 2
Am7(no 3rd)
Dadd4/A
Dmadd4/A
hon - ey, if you're need - in' a wom - an just as bad as me, ya ought - a be go -
(Oh, oh.)
Substitute Rhy. Fill 2
A5
N.C.
Pre-chorus
w/Rhy. Fig. 3
Dadd2
E5
N.C.
in'. All these cra - zy wom - en, ah, just
C
D
N.C.
Dadd2
E5
one more cra - zy night. But one night's all we're giv -
N.C.
C
D
N.C.
en, so hon - ey, leave me a - lone or, la - dy, you're stay - in' the night.
(Ah.)

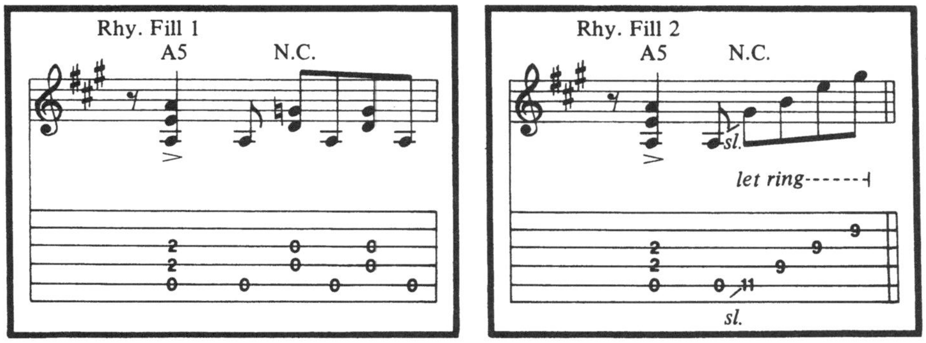
Rhy. Fill 1
A5
N.C.
Rhy. Fill 2
A5
N.C.
sl.
let ring
sl.

Guitar solo
N.C.(E5)
D
N.C.
*Tap on at indefinite point and slide up to note indicated.
(E5)
(D5)
N.C.
D.S. al Coda
let ring
Coda
(Cont. Rhy. Fig. 1)
Am/E
E5
Substitute Rhy. Fill 3
N.C.
Ooh babe, I know you're in love.
Wom-en in love.)
I know, I
Rhy. Fill 3
N.C.

Outro
E5 F♯5 F♯7sus4 G5 G6 A5
know. Ooh yeah.
Rhy. Fig. 4
w/Rhy. Fig. 4
N.C. E5 F♯5 F♯7sus4 G5 G6 A5
This wom-an in love, in love, in love, ooh
Harm.
(8va)
(end Rhy. Fig. 4)
Harm.
w/Rhy. Fig. 4 (1st 3 bars only)
N.C. E5 F♯5 F♯7sus4 G5 G6 A5
yeah. Ah, ah, ah. Ah, ah, ah. Ooh yeah.
w/Rhy. Fill 4
G5 F♯5
w/Rhy. Fig. 4 (1st 3 bars only)
E5 F♯5 F♯7sus4 G5 G6 A5
Ow! Oh yeah Oh yeah Ah.
Free time
w/Rhy. Fill 5
(Ooh.)
Rhy. Fill 4
(A5) G5 F♯5
Rhy. Fill 5
(A5)

BEAUTIFUL GIRLS

Words and Music by
EDWARD VAN HALEN, ALEX VAN HALEN,
MICHAEL ANTHONY and DAVID LEE ROTH

Tune down ½ step:
⑥ = E♭ ③ = G♭
⑤ = A♭ ② = B♭
④ = D♭ ① = E♭

side,__ on top o' the world,_____ oh yeah.__ She had a drink in her hand, she had her toes in the sand, and whoa,__ what a beau-ti-ful girl,_____ ah yeah.__ What a sweet talk-in' hon-ey, with a lit-tle bit o' mon-ey, she turn_ your head a-round._ Crea-ture

Beautiful Girls - 10 - 2

from the sea with the looks to me like she'd like to fool a - round. What a
P.M. P.M. P P P.M. P.M. P.M. sl.
N.C.
snap-py lit - tle mam-my, gon-na keep her pap - py hap - py and ac - com - pa - ny me to the ends of the
P.M. P P.M. sl.
earth, ah yeah. That's what I said.
Chorus
N.C. E5 F♯5 G5
Here I am, ain't no
P.M. P P P.M. sl. sl.
N.C. A5 B5 C5
man of the world, no.
N.C. E5 F♯5 G5
All I need is a
N.C. A5 B5 C5
beau-ti - ful girl.
sl.

G5
C5
D5
N.C.
Ah, yeah!
(Beau - ti - ful girls.)
(Spoken:) Come here, hon - ey. C' - mon, c' - mon.
Well, I'm a
2nd Verse
N.C.
bum in the sun and I'm hav - in' fun, and I know you know I got no spe - cial plans.
slight P.M.
(Spe - cial plans.)
All the
trem. bar.
*Depress bar before striking note.
bills are paid, I got it made in the shade and all I n - nee - need is the
slight P.M.

A5/F♯
wom - an. (Un - der - stand?) What a
slight P.M.
sl. sl. P P
B5
sweet talk - in' hon-ey with a lit - tle bit o' mon - ey, she turn your head a - round. A crea - ture
P.M.
Chorus
N.C. E5 F♯5 G5
from the sea with the looks to me like she'd like to fool a - round. Here I am, ain't no
N.C. A5 B5 C5
N.C. E5 F♯5 G5
N.C. A5 B5 C5
man of the world, no. All I need is a beau - ti - ful girl.
H P sl.

G5 C5 D5 B5
Ah, yeah! Beau - ti - ful girl.
Oh! Come this way, babe.
P.M. P.M. P.M.
trem. bar. semi-harm.
Guitar solo
A.H. (15ma)
N.C.(F♯5)
trem. bar.
A.H. pitch: E
Full
N.C.
E5 N.C.
Sit - down right here.
Ooh la la!
Harm.
trem. bar.

(Spoken:) I think I got it now.
Now, I'm-a
3rd Verse
N.C.
sea - side sit - tin', just - a smok - in' and - a drink - in', I'm ring - side, on top o' the world,
uh!
(Top o' the world.)
I got a
drink in my hand, I got my toes in the sand, all I need is a beau - ti - ful girl,
P.M.
slight P.M.
semi-harm.
Harm.
(15ma)
sl.
H
P
1/2

uh!
(Beau - ti - ful girl.)
Harm. (8va)
Oh yeah.
P.M.
Harm.
Chorus
N.C. E5 F♯5 G5
N.C. A5 B5 C5
N.C. E5 F♯5 G5
Here I am, ain't no man of the world, no. All I need is a
sl.
N.C. A5 B5 C5
G5 C5 D5 E5 N.C.
beau - ti - ful girl. Ah yeah!
(Beau - ti - ful girls.)
(Spoken:) I ain't lyin' to
rake
reverse rake
P.M.
D5 A5 E5 D5
Voc. Fig. 1
ya. Nothin' else I need.
Ah yeah! Beau - ti - ful girls.
Set yourself on down.
Ah

w/Voc. Fig. 1 (9 times)
A5
N.C.(E5)
D5
trem. pick.
(Spoken:) C'm here, baby. C'm here.
trem. bar
What's your name, honey? What's your... Hey, hey, where you goin'?
trem. bar
Hey!
Hey!
trem. bar.
Hey, babe, wait...

73

I love 'em! I need 'em!

Can't do with-out 'em! No!

Ah—

w/Voc. Fig. 1

yeah! Beau-ti-ful girls.

*Substitute half rest for last 2 beats. **Kissing sound.

Beautiful Girls - 10 - 10

GUITAR TAB GLOSSARY

TABLATURE EXPLANATION
TAB illustrates the six strings of the guitar.
Notes and chords are indicated by the placement of fret numbers on each string.

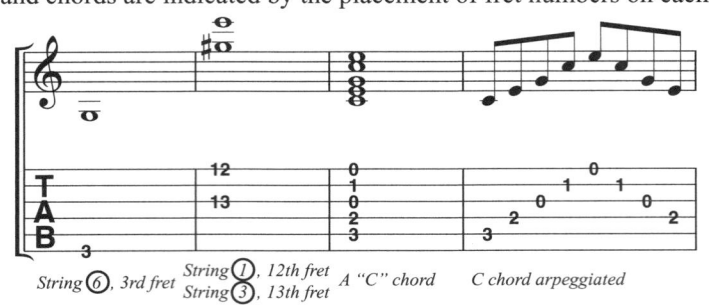

String ⑥, 3rd fret   String ①, 12th fret   A "C" chord   C chord arpeggiated
                      String ③, 13th fret

BENDING NOTES

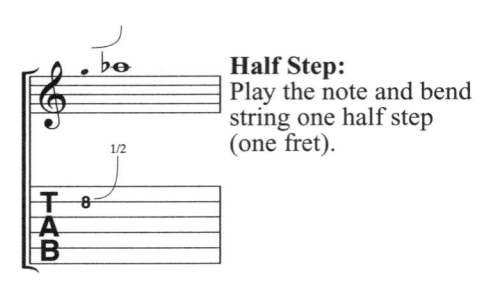

Half Step: Play the note and bend string one half step (one fret).

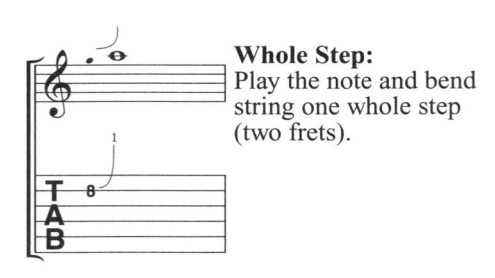

Whole Step: Play the note and bend string one whole step (two frets).

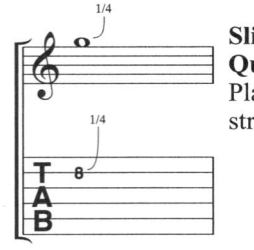

Slight Bend/Quarter-Tone Bend: Play the note and bend string sharp.

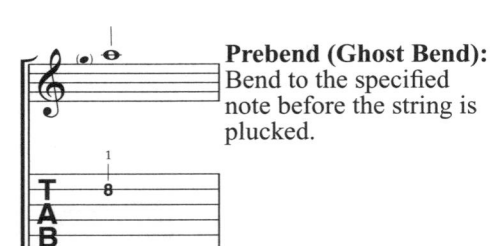

Prebend (Ghost Bend): Bend to the specified note before the string is plucked.

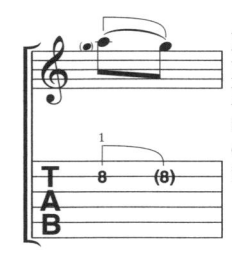

Prebend and Release: Play the already-bent string, then immediately drop it down to the fretted note.

Unison Bend: Play both notes and immediately bend the lower note to the same pitch as the higher note.

Bend and Release: Play the note and bend to the next pitch, then release to the original note. Only the first note is attacked.

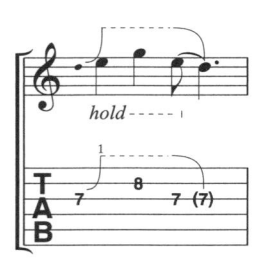

Bends Involving More Than One String: Play the note and bend the string while playing an additional note on another string. Upon release, relieve the pressure from the additional note allowing the original note to sound alone.

Bends Involving Stationary Notes: Play both notes and immediately bend the lower note up to pitch. Release bend as indicated.

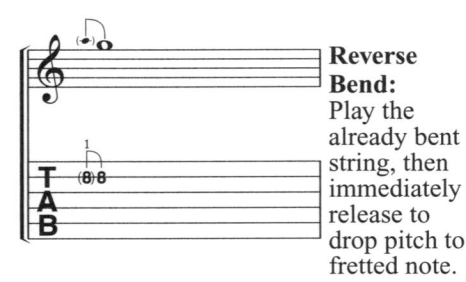

Reverse Bend: Play the already bent string, then immediately release to drop pitch to fretted note.

Unison Bend: Play both notes and immediately bend the lower note to the same pitch as the higher note.

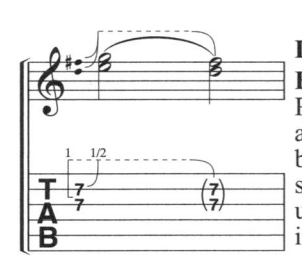

Double Note Bend: Play both notes and immediately bend both strings simultaneously up the indicated intervals.

ARTICULATIONS

Hammer On (Ascending Slur): Play the lower note, then "hammer" your finger to the higher note. Only the first note is plucked.

Pull Off (Descending Slur): Play the higher note with your first finger already in position on the lower note. Pull your finger off the first note with a strong downward motion that plucks the string—sounding the lower note.

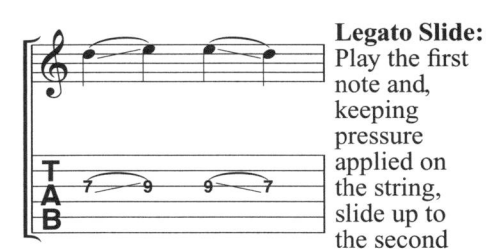

Legato Slide: Play the first note and, keeping pressure applied on the string, slide up to the second note. The diagonal line shows that it is a slide and not a hammer-on or a pull-off.

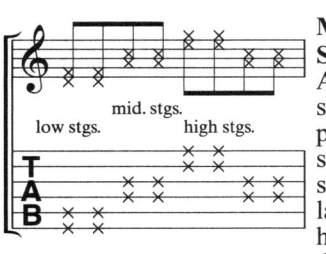

Muted Strings: A percussive sound is produced by striking the strings while laying the fret hand across them.

Palm Mute: The notes are muted (muffled) by placing the palm of the pick hand lightly on the strings, just in front of the bridge.

Left Hand Hammer: Using only the left hand, hammer on the first note played on each string.

Glissando: Play note and slide in specified direction.

Bend and Tap Technique: Play note and bend to specified interval. While holding bend, tap onto fret indicated with a "t."

Fretboard Tapping: Tap onto the note indicated by the "t" with a finger of the pick hand, then pull off to the following note held by the fret hand.

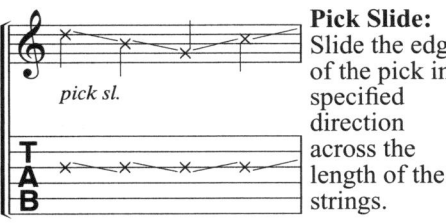

Pick Slide: Slide the edge of the pick in specified direction across the length of the strings.

Tremolo Picking: The note or notes are picked as fast as possible.

Trill: Hammer on and pull off consecutively and as fast as possible between the original note and the grace note.

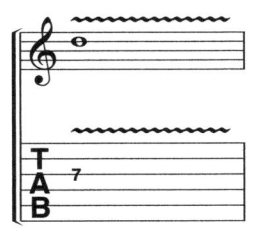

Vibrato: The pitch of a note is varied by a rapid shaking of the fret-hand finger, wrist, and forearm.

Accent: Notes or chords are to be played with added emphasis.

Staccato (Detached Notes): Notes or chords are to be played about half their noted value and with separation.

HARMONICS

Natural Harmonic: A finger of the fret hand lightly touches the string at the note indicated in the TAB and is plucked by the pick producing a bell-like sound called a harmonic.

Artificial Harmonic: Fret the note at the first TAB number, lightly touch the string at the fret indicated in parens (usually 12 frets higher than the fretted note), then pluck the string with an available finger or your pick.

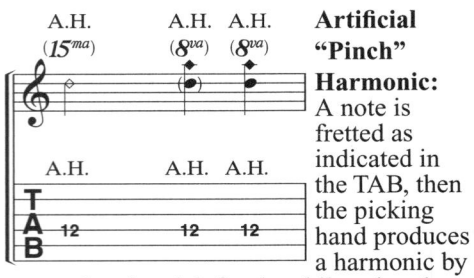

Artificial "Pinch" Harmonic: A note is fretted as indicated in the TAB, then the picking hand produces a harmonic by squeezing the pick firmly while using the tip of the index finger in the pick attack. If parenthesis are found around the fretted note, it does not sound. No parenthesis means both the fretted note and the A.H. are heard simultaneously.

RHYTHM SLASHES

Strum Marks/Rhythm Slashes: Strum with the indicated rhythm pattern. Strum marks can be located above the staff or within the staff.

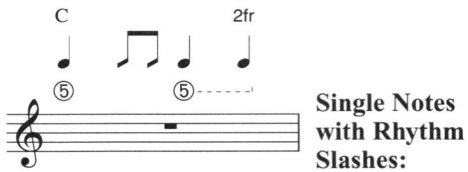

Single Notes with Rhythm Slashes: Sometimes single notes are incorporated into a strum pattern. The circled number below is the string and the fret number is above.

TREMOLO BAR

Specified Interval: The pitch of a note or chord is lowered to the specified interval and then return as indicated. The action of the tremolo bar is graphically represented by the peaks and valleys of the diagram.

Unspecified Interval: The pitch of a note or chord is lowered, usually very dramatically, until the pitch of the string becomes indeterminate.

PICK DIRECTION

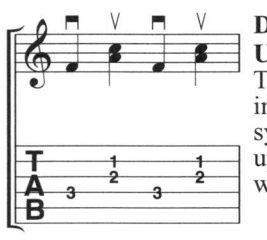

Downstrokes and Upstrokes: The downstroke is indicated with this symbol (⊓) and the upstroke is indicated with this (V).